· H A N D M A D E   P A P E R ·

poems by

PATRICIA BARONE

Minnesota Voices Project Number 60

NEW RIVERS PRESS 1994

Cover, "Waterfowl II," by Elizabeth Bachhuber
Elizabeth Bachhuber, a professor of art at Weimar University in Germany, has had
shows throughout Europe and the United States. Among her many honors are a German
Kunstsonds national grant, a P.S. 1 studio residency grant in New York, and a Na-
tional Endowment for the Arts fellowship in sculpture.

The publication of *Handmade Paper* has been made possible by generous grants from
the Dayton Hudson Foundation on behalf of Dayton's and Target Stores, the Jerome
Foundation, the Metropolitan Regional Arts Council (from an appropriation by the
Minnesota Legislature), the North Dakota Council on the Arts, the South Dakota Arts
Council, and the James R. Thorpe Foundation.

Additional support has been provided by the General Mills Foundation, Land o' Lakes,
Inc., Liberty State Bank, the McKnight Foundation, the Star Tribune/Cowles Media
Company, the Tennant Company Foundation, and the contributing members of New
Rivers Press. New Rivers Press is a member agency of United Arts.

New Rivers Press books are distributed by

The Talman Company
131 Spring Street, Suite 201 E-N
New York NY 10012

Handmade Paper has been manufactured in the United States of America for New
Rivers Press, 420 N. 5th Street/Suite 910, Minneapolis, MN 55401. First Edition.

I dedicate this work to the inspiration
of this work—artists: photographers, gardeners,
musicians, sculptors, writers, painters, and printmakers.
I particularly dedicate Handmade Paper *to the*
visual artists of my family who build their lives
on the good work of hands,
for Elizabeth Bachhuber and Christoph Rihs
for Jean and Frank Gross

ACKNOWLEDGEMENTS

Some of the poems in *Handmade Paper* have appeared in the following magazines, sometimes in an earlier version: *And Magazine, Blue Buildings, Germination, Gusto, Laughing Unicorn, Loonfeather, Mankato Poetry Review, The Next Parish Over: A Collection of Irish-American Writing* (New Rivers Press, 1993), *Onionskins, Poets On: Hurting, Poets On: Remembering, Sing Heavenly Muse!, Visions International, West End, Widener Review, Women's Quarterly Review*.

The author wishes to thank her writing group, Onionskins—members past and present—for their helpful criticism and long encouragement. And the author is grateful to her editor, Vivian Vie Balfour, whose insight and germinal questions stimulated new work.

CONTENTS

· LANDSCAPES LIKE HOME OR THE BODY ·

IN LIFE

And the aunts and uncles
who climbed in the upstairs windows
are gone. Someone left a mandolin.
It's all up for
Aunt Claire, Aunt Ruth, Uncle Alois.

No more coffee, or gin, no bills
of lading, invitations, hummingbirds
in morning glories, no more mud.

The nieces and the nephews with their children
eat watermelon, spitting seeds
on the graves of the uncles and the aunts.

They mean no disrespect,
they are in life—
rowing across a river,
when the current makes it easier
to drift ten miles down stream
than reach the other shore.

And the boat is so full of their things:
refrigerators, comforters, mouse traps,
coals, bandages, wine, cashews and rakes.
So full of retorts, reports, weeping,
so very full of it, just full of it!
So full up to the *teeth* with juicy black
grapes, gripes, braces, races, and schnapps.
And their shoes are so full of their toes.

INHERITANCE

In the middle
of my thirtieth year,

in a frame house
we didn't mean to buy
across from Kreuzer's farm,

all May I woke by dawn
wanting to grow corn.

A dream told me to plant potatoes.
in the gibbous moon's waxing shine.

I knew just what to do
preparing soil, I'd haul

black manure across the highway,
red blood meal, white bone meal

from the feed store, as if
born in the country, though I never
owned a houseplant in the city.

It was just that the landscape
looked familiar, though disguised

by lawn we ripped from one half acre,
to beard the backyard slope with peas.

By June I saw the face upon our field:
Great-grandfather Ryan, his profile—

a land-work of hoeing, ridges in the soil—
telling me to listen for the Evergreen
corn, it grew so fast I heard the silk spin

his image through my hands.

THE CARD PLAYERS

After a painting by Cezanne:

*The only game is "Schafkopf,"
(Sheephead) in Mayville, Wisconsin
one hundred years after Cezanne
painted his three-handed game*

These regulars, their feet fit
the same worn places on the floor
beneath the foursquare table.

The kibitzer's obliged
to look amused and knowing:
Uncle Chas smokes a pipe he likes to point as

Aunt Maxine, with better hands than she admits,
refuses to pick up the blind.
"I'd rather lose one chip than two," says she,
"when we play double on the bump."

Cezanne's habitues go on
playing for centuries,
even when transplanted
to Mayville after the fish fry

where Uncle Alphonse, Uncle Alois, Uncle Edward
depend on each other to "schmiere"
(put more points on the trump).

"Schiess mal los!" (Shoot! Let's go!),
says Aunt Romana when they play
too slowly, "aber nicht in der hosen,"
which means—but not in your pants.

There's no unseemly display.
Cezanne's miller still wears his smock
and the pharmacist, his white coat.

Neither conceal black queens
within their roomy sleeves.
The seat of the bank clerk's suit

is used to him, is polished, and his hat
is thumbed down on the brim
to its usual angle.

The table where the aunts and uncles
deal good hands, bad hands, is rubbed by their hands
to a patina—better than good luck.

LAKESCAPE/LANDSCAPE, ESCAPE

for my cousins, Betsy Litke and Nancy Massman

1.

In the naive painting—
oil on pinewood—
Great-uncle Hugo
held a rigid fish,
tail down, scissor mouth
open at his elbow.

Great-aunt Marie always cautioned,
"Keep your collar buttoned, and
remember you're the principal!"
He took his other Shakespeare
      in the boat.

Was that why he painted himself,
upon a tiny dock, receding
like railroad tracks behind his boots
and far below his fishing rod,
which poked an improbable sunset?

2.

When young enough to have a fluent brush
I turned Hugo's lakescape over
to paint my own landscape on the back—
coal hills, limned in gold.

Was it good? I didn't know.
      Was I?
I didn't know that either.
How could it be, I be—
good, if the doing was so easy?

Though afraid to stake a claim
on my own painting,
            for praise,
I loaned it to my teacher
            who lost it—
along with Uncle Hugo's alter ego.
            I gave us both away.

3.

I recall how my lost river,
snaking with unsentimental
precision between ridges,
was like Uncle Hugo's net—
            a gift.

Now either side of our picture
against whatever wall—
is the right side.

The dock projects
just a little ways
into the repetitious water.

REUNION

*You will come at sunset
to pitch a tent on common ground,
near the large flat rock—
familiar as your table.
You are ready now for the family.*

The next reunion picnic
Uncle Alois is in danger,
Fading past an oak tree where he plays
Pinochle, and the cousins will not hold still

Under multiple exposures of
The yearly portrait.

Your youngest brother Tom—so fast
He passes into death out of growing pains.

His hair spikes up, slicks down, falls out
While you set the dilled beans before him.

It's time to relax, your legs extended.
The west sun slants so hard, you're left

One foot in afternoon, the other
In nightshade, half home, but where?

In the dark room negative you never see
Light develops where the shadow is most deep.

IN THE ABSENCE OF
GREAT-UNCLE JOHN CUTHBERT

Great-uncle John Cuthbert smiles in the family portrait. No one else is smiling. Was it soon after this that he left Appleton, Wisconsin, for Mexico? He sent them a postcard:

Dear Mother, Father, Robert, Dudley, Liz, and Kitty,

I've found a job in railroad. The pay is good and I'll send some soon.

Love,
John

That's the last they ever heard from him. (Although Grandma Lizzie, when she was in her eighties, insisted he had wired the St. Louis Station.) At barely thirteen, Lizzie inherited her brother's chore—fetching her father daily from the tavern. John Cuthbert, Sr., played church organ for the Catholics and Lutherans alike, and took in a few private students: That the end result of a degree from Trinity College. To fill young John's empty room and bring in money, the Cuthberts gave room and board to Thomas Henry Ryan, a law student. In their engagement photo, Tom and Lizzie are quite unlike most Victorian coupled arrangements: he is the one standing, his moustache cocked up in a grin. She sits, one wrist delicately bent over the antlers sprouting from the settee. Her eyes find nothing funny in trusting so completely.

PHOTO OF ELIZABETH CUTHBERT AND THOMAS RYAN,
ABOUT 1897

AUNT WINIFRED RYAN

Aunt Winifred Ryan, big-boned and freckled, stares us down from her photograph. Her hair is pulled back so tight her scalp shows through. For forty years she lived on the farm with her brothers Malachy and Dan. The nieces and nephews would coax her to lift her skirt and do a jig—dancing past everyone else's strength or gaiety. Then she'd go back to picking worms from the cabbage, breaking ground for turnips. Just before Prohibition, her sister Nell ran a tavern; Winifred spanked the children who bought candy there.

After her brothers died, she lived by herself in a white frame house on the edge of Kaukauna. She had a black wood-burning stove that she used to make an endless supply of thin gingersnaps. To a child who was unafraid of her, she'd say, "Your mother can bring you round again. You have a little spirit and a tongue in your head."

AUNT MAGGIE

Aunt Maggie Powers was seduced and abandoned by Harry Houdini in the family story. His name was Erich Weiss then, the son of an immigrant Hungarian rabbi. And Maggie went to Saint Mary's Catholic Church. One day when she was about seventeen, Uncle Malachy and Uncle Dan might have come in from the farm for a day of buying and selling. And she may have slipped away from them to go to the forbidden Appleton Bijou Theater where Erich first performed on the trapeze. In the photo, she has large eyes with paper-thin bruised circles underneath, black hair, and a victim smile. What did she think of his transformation to Houdini? Upside down in water, strait-jacketed, roped and weighed? He later said he owed his escapes to great strength and bowed legs. He married Wilhemina and Maggie married a man who drank before he beat her.

In real memory, we have a winter afternoon and an image of her hands scrabbling at a window. We stand on a porch in December, the swing covered with snow. My little brother Eddie holds a frozen fruitcake in one mitten and I grip his other hand as we stare back at the old lady: Her face is pressed against the glass and I imagine rainbow bubbles rising, one by one, from the O of her open mouth. Then one colored ball falls and she disappears from view. We peer through the window to see her kneeling, trying to pick up the glass slivers of a broken ornament. All this time our mother has been trying the back door. When she returns, she turns us around and gives us a shove toward the steps. "Winifred and Dan must have locked her in. What a pity."

UNCLE AUGIE

Uncle August, natty in the photo, drives and wears a four-in-hand. Or does he sport a cravat, his vehicle a surrey? I don't know why we put him, a gentleman and country doctor, in the family story of the ridiculous disappearance:

 One spring day Uncle Augie drove his carriage to the bridge. On the Rock River bank, they found his pocket watch, morning coat, spats, and creased trousers. He'd left in his long-thighed, purple-striped bathing costume, yet somehow reached the Fox by August. In December when the river froze, we'd see him caught in the locks, his moustache sticking up. We'd boil some melting water, which made his moustache droop. He liked to look lugubrious. In the summer he'd be a goggle-eyed merman, floating under the pier, his sideburns woven with lake sedge and moss. When his travels involved him in the plumbing, Father would roar, "Is nothing sacred!" So we never did tell about the time Uncle Augie fought an alligator to the death in the Chicago sewer system.

THE STORY TELLERS

for Claire Ryan Ratfield

The Lives of Grownups, like illustrated primers,
                      were easy to explain:
"What's your mom like when she's mad?
                         Mine curls her tongue,
up behind her teeth like a sausage."
My mother served her life up
Sundays with "Heavenly Hash,"
telling the same stories over till
we'd chorus her unchanging lines:
"Romana Josephine Teresa had a child

conceived in Oklahoma, born in Texas!"
Cousin Norma went with Willard thirty years:
"Well, pardon my long white gloves!"
         We never doubted, never failed
to listen every Sunday for the way—
Grandma, "feisty" in the hospital,
cut geriatric restraints
        with a bread knife,
choosing to come home and die.
        "I'll die too,"

said Great-aunt Win, trying to steal Grandma's glory,
but Aunt Pat snorted, "You're too cheap. You just
paid your coal bill. You'll last till spring."
Uncle Frank went out and got a haircut,
as his wife, Aunt Claire, lay dying
When she rallied, he said,
"Guess I wasted my money."
Which is not to say the family's understated:
                     Take Uncle Tom,

who, in World War II, saved German children from the Russians
by hiding them in a castle. Twenty years later they sent him
                              a Mercedes.
By then Uncle Tom's Irish mug, sold to Hollywood,
filled the last screen in *Armored Command:*
                    "The cameraman didn't
think much of Howard Keel. And Tina Louise
                              kissed me on my—
                    lips! Where else?"

Uncle Tom's daughter, Claire, is a stand-up
                              comic in L.A.
Her routine includes Paddy's visit to Mike's wake,
where he trips on the grand piano, and says to the widow,
"Mary, I never realized—he had such a fine set of teeth!"
Which reminds me how many family stories turn upon
death. Family voices seldom keen,
                    though nostalgia is
Aunt Nelly's soda bread minus cream of tartar.

As Grandpa Ryan was fond of saying: "If you're going
to go, be on your way, don't stand in the doorway all night."

FROM THE PENCIL BOX
OF MANY COLORS

Here's the sun hat Great-aunt Cresentia
wore—it's come to rest as she has
in the present. We so resent the dead.
Alive, we're erasing and revising.

The pencil box of red leather
holds every color in the world almost,
the curlings fall inside the sharpener.
In my cave, I eat my bun, shading in
the chair where Gram sits eating semmeln.
The sun is in the sun room, a striped awning,
My father is at war and Granddad is dying.

The purple clematis vine comes
out my pencil thick—like fingers,
To make the flower mouth bigger, I shade
the throat. Sore, say ah—the doctor
opens the gate, goes under the trellis
with tape and fever syrup for my brother.
Our robin croaks, my brother cries. I bury
feathers trapped in sand. Ash Wednesday
our father wears soot on his forehead.

Summer at the Appleton station, Aunt Pat
waits with the Buick, for taking me across
the bumpety bridge in charcoal gray,
strokes of Prussian blue—the Fox River
toward Neenah, Menasha, Combined Locks.
The paper mills puffing white clouds
and Grandma divides the last cream puff,
Aunt reads the *New Yorker,* and I sip 7-Up
during *Parsifal,* some dancers carry parasols
for Billy the Kid, toe points in magenta,
without my brother who died at home.

From under currant jelly in the pantry
shelf paper unrolls on the kitchen table.
I draw Aunt Pat swimming in the river
the time she found a body in the dam.
As Grandma's spice cake is drawn
from the oven, Aunt Pat is reaching up
for the light switch, for heaven,
and she falls and doesn't stop falling
till she's a child in her home again.

APPENZELL LANDSCAPE

When I dream of leaf pile houses—
small enough to leapfrog,
snug against my back—
I travel to sleep,
and return as Gulliver:
        a river
hums my arm,
grown to mountain range
under head, perched above
like an Appenzell dwelling—
squat, so the hills seem higher.

Scaled like a Chinese scroll,
ridges tuck neat.
Nothing recedes and even
the narrow gauge train
passes, shaves the barn's
moss roof tile.

Plateaus behind me, I enter
this valley no longer
than breath, or stride
past knolls, rumped,
split at the crotch by a forest—
a landscape like home or the body.

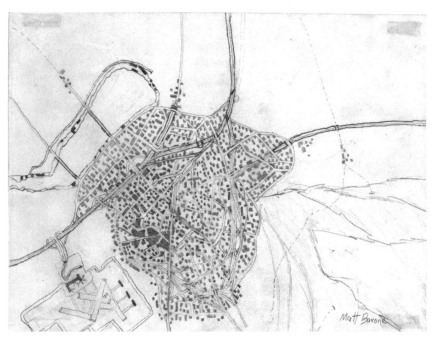

"CITY FREEWAY,"
PENCIL DRAWING
BY MATT BARONE, 1990

"SELF PORTRAIT OF CHRISTOPH RIHS,"
PHOTOGRAPH
BY CHRISTOPH GUNIG IN *ZEIT RAUM* BY CHRISTOPH RIHS

MAPS

My son draws maps—under/overpasses coiling
the central cities, then straightening to zoom
past the suburbs. His pencil lingers
on knotted arteries, I love to see
him—the slight swelling as the blood
flows through his temple pulse.

At ten I drew trees from the bottom down,
    making roots plunge rocks
to underground rivers, and my life
was a story I told myself while listening

to the Friday Night Fights: A right to the jaw—
as I shaded in the left side of the trunk—
    a kidney punch—
the Madison Square Garden crowd
booed as I colored the leaves.

"Do you really like boxing?"
the aunts and uncles asked me.
Like it? It was what I heard
drawing and eating potato chips.

Like it? Did I like the oilcloth
on the kitchen table, oatmeal,
    spankings or cigars?
Grownups did what they did in the world,
it wasn't up to kids to like it.

Nothing so infuriates a child
as a grownup saying "I don't know,"
    Grownups do *so* know—
even before the child was born, how much
time before anything happens!

"Maybe you'll be a traffic engineer,
or an artist like Uncle Christoph,"
I tell my son, and he thinks I'm crazy
but maybe right and that's scary.

Children think parents' lives
take place in a different geography—
    surveyed block by block
    and house by house,

Like the taxi driver's map book—
with numbers at top, side, and bottom
sending kids to the past,
    present, future—

all tomorrow stretching
ahead and coming to an end—
    in a bottomless canyon,
or a foreign country like Canada—
if that's part of the story
    any grownup
knows and won't tell kids
out of meanness.

Hadn't all adults arrived
at their own spots on the map?
Wasn't Uncle Chas the joker, Uncle Todd
good at getting in the paper, and Aunt Ruth
an orchid grower, our mother our mother?

In the country they ruled,
wasn't everyone fixed the way they were?
Back then I was sure—I didn't know
there never was a map with more vulnerable
rivers, than my own body's pulse, it
carried the cargo of the heart.

· WRITING ON HANDMADE PAPER ·

"ROCK RIVER PART I"
FROM A TRIPTYCH PENCIL DRAWING
BY ELIZABETH BACHHUBER, 1978

WRITING ON HANDMADE PAPER

I. THE PROBLEM

She can't write, so she consults
a dream book, then can't remember
whose dreams she should be having.

＊

She can't write, but composts words
stolen from *Time* magazine,
some on the outside like rind,
some inside like ersatz seeds.

＊

She tries to guess the secret
word for the duck's magic dollar.
What comes is "probate." Groucho grins.
It means she has been writing
someone else's will.

＊

She'd like to be the child with adult knowledge
of number, pointing in turn to each
countable thing, reserving incantations.

＊

She's sleeping, then stumbling
out of bed when the baby cries,
and back to bed forgetting
an almost dream: leaning over
and unable—
as if at the edge of orgasm—
to go in. Is it a well?
No reflection in the water.

She's sleeping when she wants
to be wakeful, and wakeful
for sleep and coming back from sleep
with no shining fish at all.

II. THE PROCESS

Leaving herself is like dropping cherries to the middle of half-firmed jello: The top closes over. She discards the persona of her old concerns—Columbine, Cinderella, Punchinella, The Witch. When they go, they take back her gestures, her choreography, and she's afraid: How will she move her body? Columbine dances off with the legs; Cinderella, her arms around the pumpkin, never waves. Punchinella peels off her smile, and The Witch takes her heart for an apple. She covers her eyes as, rolling the canvas up upon its stretchers, they remove her landscape. Still, she wants to believe her company isn't lost, only disbanded—gone into desultory odd jobs like any out-of-work actors.

This dismissal of her formerly "serious" life should have depressed her. But she has become immune to negative feelings—like the housewife in old Colgate commercials who simpered with her child behind the invisible cavity shield. Soon her shield dissolves, leaving no boundary between her body and the world.

Now that her body is no longer separate, neither is her mind. Unable to work, she sleeps, resting her arm and cheek on the paper she'd placed there for writing. She can feel the sheet expand, then split along hairline fractures between strata of rag stock. Her arm, which has also gone to sleep, loses its link with her shoulder and swells into a mountain at the top of paper foothills. This distortion of relative size seems, somehow, connected to a new and more diffuse sense of touch.

She awakes with a sense of wasted time, as palpable as the shifted block of winter sunshine on her desk: She feels there are spaces inside her unused paper.

The needles of blood that follow
the rejoining of arm to shoulder,
can't knit her back together.

She uncramps her hand and writes, "I have to find myself." Cliches tick in her mind like incisors on a spoon while someone is slurping soup. Other people's mouth sounds go right to the cringing center of her cervix—like a tight diaphragm: sexual in a most unpleasant way—the baby pulling at the breast and the man saying, "You must have healed by now." Too many people want her body.

Nights, the baby cries just as she feels herself sinking into familiar landscapes. Soon, in the intervals, she no longer submerges herself, but remains suspended without dreaming, her thoughts the color of tepid water.

It's easy to miss dream erasures from her protected sleep. Unlike the dreams of her former life, she spins no imagery. She strives to loose the treadles for vague patterns pushing up through thwarted weaving.

She needs to pull loops into needle points for her tapestry of minute connections. But her hands are too clumsy to even pull wool through the eye. She hopes for new threads or other tributaries—the sort that form by themselves: new veins came to her pelvis during pregnancy.

> Stitches in layers of skin
> the birth canal newly tightened
> like a drawstring bag.
>
> She must go on repairing
> her layers as she can,
> just lying here become
> like felt, interlock her own
> fibers with steam in this hot house.
>
> And if the layers disappear
> like dissolving vaginal stitches,
>   what then?
>
> *To dream, you need layers:*
> She hasn't time.
> The compost can mix itself.
> Earthworms, up and down
> through hair, squash, and oatmeal,
> leave castings and transform
> the space that enters them.

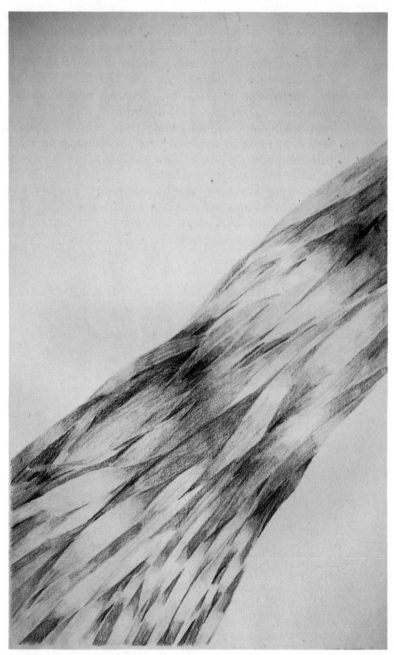

"ROCK RIVER PART II"
FROM A TRIPTYCH PENCIL DRAWING
BY ELIZABETH BACHHUBER, 1978

But she can't break through and can't take in   hardpan.

Every time there is   a metamorphic upthrust, tongue of lava—

she's told to get back in bed. "When you get up too fast, you faint."

It's good to accept the necessary   weakness   and peaceful

        and good to feed the baby   she loves.

    Baby cries: The milk sacs fill.   The milk "lets down."

She has done nothing   to call it forth   so while the baby sucks

she's free to imagine   another task: herself in summer.

standing in a stream with many women.   She helps to hold

a mash of mulberry, bark, and cotton

                              in a screen beneath the water.

    In this way, the rag stock is filtered and made finer.

    Some of the pulp breaks loose from the screen and floats down river.

All at once her arms are heavy at her sides. She wants to lay the screen

down, lay herself down on the current

be carried along on the water.

                    She drifts on the surface, wanting
                    to dream of a layered pool:
                    Algae on top,
                    as silt settles out,
                    warm in the shallows
                    with larger
                    fish now and then
                    in deeper cold behind a rock.

She is as empty, as flattened as the womb that let the baby go.

Now it wants the mother, enclosed in afterbirth.

The womb let the baby go,   and wants to be filled again.

Layering cells, a lining to be sloughed.

Until the baby came, the womb   filled and emptied apart

from the body above it   below it.

Now when the baby sucks, she feels herself tighten below,

and it hurts and is a pleasure, and the man is the same

hurt and spreading pleasure in her body.

Soon she thinks she is
all milk.

The baby's cries make
milk: Too much won't flow.

The veins of her breast are blue.
Soon she'll have milk fever.

Sliced through, she would be
white, crisp and cold like ice cream:

vein-less, with just burning to connect
her breasts to the rest of her body.

Growing up, she used a narrow milk chute
for looking out and wriggling in.
When the milkman left the bottles on the stoop,
cream froze, pushing up the top.

Thawing milk rose up round cream and flowed,
down the sides, so sweet upon her tongue.

Her sleep is thick   so   sluggish and she falls   slowly

        through it.   Something in her once   had tried to rise.

        Now she rests as

                        she falls

and because her skin fills with air
                    like a parachute,

                she can't leave herself behind.

In this way, she lands. The curtain comes down. Backstage, the actors are

        employed again. She notices they're wearing other costumes.

                She's pleased to see that no one needs her body.

                At peace, she admires the sword-swallower for his

        inner balance: He keeps himself together with each thrust.

                Like the magician's lady   she can fold herself whole

        into the smallest space, where she escapes dismemberment.

                Conjurers with rope tricks practice

sleight of hand. I can do that too, she thinks

and maybe with real snakes.

At last in her own dream
of swimming the cotton-mouth river,
she keeps near the farmland shore.
It's spring, and seeds in sacks
wait for the land to dry.

Along the outlet stream
from an old shale fault,
layers touch but do not mix
topsoil and drainage gravel.
She wants to hear a garden—
over-ground stems make roots
if only they touch down.

At last in her own work
she is soaking rag and hemp
till their fibers fit together
as hill-country landscape is filled in
with trees and rock outcroppings.

As she works, she uses
(breathing like a swimmer over fish)
a mantra she's never been taught.
Asleep, she listens for her child
and sometimes wakes just moments
before the cries begin:

She is making paper.
The watermark left from
the pressure of her hands is hers.

"ROCK RIVER PART III"
FROM A TRIPTYCH PENCIL DRAWING
BY ELIZABETH BACHHUBER, 1978

· PORTRAITS OF WOMEN ·

RELECTIONS ON
A YOUNG WOMAN MENDING

a painting by PISSARRO

Hands gather cloth. You seem
to exhale as the needle
locks the stitch to dip again.

Have you really gone
to dream at the edge of sleep?
Or are you wholly breathing
in the moment's peace-
work, a steady rhythm,
pull of the present easing?

A gentle repetition is the only way
            to float this room
just beyond the corner of my eye.
The walls expand, contract.
My shoulders too, seem to melt

into the space where sunlight whites
the quiet, molds the floor and table
to your back and waiting.

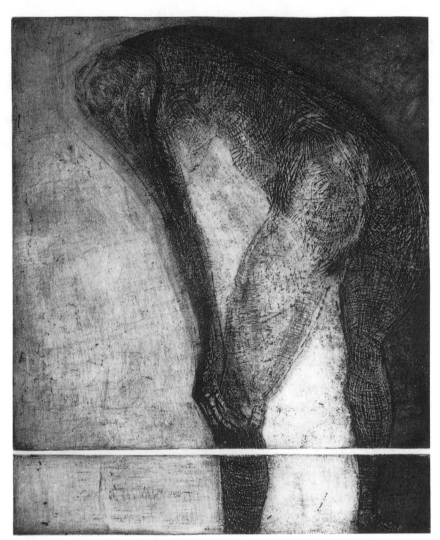

"THE SWIMMER,"
INTAGLIO
BY PATRICIA BARONE, 1972

ON THE PATIENCE
OF SHOULDERS

1.

The swimmer revolved
her shoulders 500 times

in just one lap.
Her shoulder met her neck

in a runnel of pain.
From her shoulder, a whine—

like an angry mosquito:
Pain is one connection, and

the essence of the shoulder
is connection.

Do shoulders want this?
Are they wings
diverted into arms?

2.

The purpose of the arm
is bent around the elbow.

Status for the elbow comes
from being in the middle.

If I release my shoulders
the breasts would be afraid

and the arms without excuse
on the hands' assembly line.

The hands would call in scabs
just to pick an apple.

The hands would tinker forever
and never let the shoulders go.

The hands want the shoulders
quiet and symmetrical.

The hands don't want
the shoulders to claim each other.

TRANSLATION
from 1968

In the past-perfect tense of fifty,
I know the conditional only.

The *pasta marinara* with *piccola* clams in '68
and the wine enabled me to speak
existantialismo with Hugo.

On the Rapido, Madrid to Paris,
I spoke of the Vietnam War
with a *Paris Soir* reporter
in French—he seemed to say
    he was for it.

While leaving the Louvre, Henri said that he
had been Edith Piaf's *docteur.* His name
was not in the phone book, but Gaylynne
said why not *"s'amusions* over *bifsteak* with
a French escort?" Gigolo was more like it:
His wallet became *perdu.*

I was glad I couldn't speak German.
Getting the verb at the end
would have given me too much time
to see what the syntax left out—

Did I imagine all we said?
Did Hugo, Henri, et cetera,
speak instead of love or artichokes?

A bookstore on the left bank sold me
Daisy Miller, who died of waiting
around in a damp Coliseum.

Had I been waiting for someone
to give me the message of my life?
There's no need to wait at twenty-five for
the future, which is always coming on.

What made me think my destiny
would come as a translation,
an illuminated footnote, or a large
ornamental letter to a foreign text?

If I truly learned a foreign language,
                would I be undeluded—
as when fending off Henri in the foyer of
                that pension?

Would I make reservations
in hotels: word-proud, always matching
subject to verb, forgetting
                my unlived life
was found in a bad translation?

A MYSTERY

with clues in italic

In my dream, I must please
          two men in two
different restaurants.

With *my husband,* I eat shrimp.
          The garlic butter
          runs from the corner of my mouth.

I excuse myself because it's time
to race to the other
table, other man, who is—
          my father.

That's not all I do, I must
save my place in line outside the bank vault
or someone will steal the jewels and silver.

When I return, my husband—
          is gone.
They even took the food away.

I hadn't time to eat.
The silver must be wedding
silver and too good
for eating every day.
That's why I'm always hungry
with nothing to lift up my food
but my own fingers.

How can I keep my place,
          eat my food,
keep my man eating
with me if I must be with father?

Did my father know
where that ivory broach
landed when it fell
from my breast?

In the grocery bag.
Then I shelved it away so well
I never found it again.

Now I never
unpack the gin and cereal,
    set the table,
move the dishes to the sink without
    wondering
who was going to steal
the jewels and silver?

If it was my husband,
that's why he left.

If it was me, and I think it was—
I could have finished the shrimp
and I could have licked my fingers.

SURFACES: WOMAN IN A MIRROR
AND IN A LANDSCAPE
hidden in a painting by William Turner

Over and over I meet my mother,
reflect my body is hers.

A middle-aged woman is
constructed in pier glass:
three ways right to left
and backwards.

She's out there—

like that landscape:
In a certain light
you'd see her too
(neutral orange bleeding
on cobalt sky).
Her separation
from the background
surprising as

me running toward me—a stranger
with no time to shift
eyes or nose hunched together.
No time to assemble a mirror face,

despite all those years as a girl—
in mirrors, our self-glazed faces,

In the weak autumn light
of a varnished forest
a woman rescues her own face,
barely.

and our bodies in fat mirrors or thin:
sucked in stomachs till they touched
back ribs, contracted buttocks

till our hips were ornamental, not
for sitting, and sidewise, we
narrowed in our looking

glasses, wavered and
almost disappeared.

         In her figure-
ground reversal,
her edges
fuzz, a scumble
of the brush,
a blurred vision—
an inverted eyelash and
angry red stains
the corner of the eye
         like weeping.

It rains when she's mad,
her tears refracted by
the setting sun.

We were encouraged to
display our favored parts:

I silvered a window, and lolled
      on the surface,
a pouf—big hair, a swipe of brow, a large
      cerise mouth: *Her tongue barely shows*
between her teeth,

Openings came to no more
than decoration.

as she tries to speak.
Her teeth are too heavy,
zinc white, cadmium.

Still, she opens her lips,
and lifts her hand.

I once went shopping
at an airport;

Clerks spread maps,
dress lengths quilted in silk.

I crawled longitudinal meridians
laying my Simplicity

pattern on the hills and valleys.
Exhausted, I would have purchased

a fine topographical
anatomy, my destination, but

Atlantis was always expensive
and never the right size.

If only she'd paint herself
bone white, and circle
each nipple in crimson,
but she is the model,
she is painted.
She is the underpainting, she
is not the painter's varnish,
not a trick
of palette knife,
not washed
in pink.

She is her own palimpsest, she
is rising to the surface, and she
is legion.

Now Turner's landscape explodes into light-
portraits of women
holding copper against their bodies:
The sun is caught and they throw it back
from their weapons,
not their shields.
Burn the water! Burn the sky!
Their focus is too good
to be anger only.

"PORTRAITS OF WOMEN,"
MONOPRINT
BY PATRICIA BARONE, 1972

BEFORE SHE COULD DRAW
A WHITE STALLION

The white horse has
one wild and wicked eye,
says the farmer, see it wander,
        a wall eye, guess the poor
beast sees two of everything, or more, take care
Go through the gate—don't climb over
the split fir fence
into the west
pasture. I don't know
what he'd do if you intruded.

She climbs a ladder to the barn loft where hay is stacked in rectangular loaves, piled one upon the other in the mows, spilling into the nave. She peers out through an opening in the west-facing peaked dormer.

The horse stands still except for its tail
whisking from flank to flank, he curves his neck—
sighting down his back, catching her.

What if she slipped on the shiny straw,
what if she slid so fast she couldn't grasp
                        the punky
sides opening to sky and ground
                —a passage for
birds, not made to keep a heavier
        human body in?

She'd fall and no calm trajectory
would keep her from landing
near his hooves.

With her back resting upon one bale, her feet upon another, she looks up at the vault of the roof, its jointed supports feathering into the mitered crossbeams of the loft. A few wrens fly through the chaff dust.

A discarded patchwork quilt, tacked high under the skylight window to catch the whiting of swifts or swallows, twists with the tail of a down draft, billows and is still.

In a dream between sleep
and waking, she falls
suspended in her patchwork hammock:
The ancient calico tears, and she plummets gently,
as if with grain down the chute.

Down she slides into a mix of manure and straw on the lower level next to the pasture. A few mice burrow. Sheets and ropes of dusty cobwebs hang with the weight of bird dung on the damp plaster.

A gallop in the farm yard—past the bolted door,
and a bull from his stall in the back
bellows and the caged small dogs
start yipping.

Chickens startle at the thudding. When she enters their wire mesh enclosure, burgundy Bresse, and speckled Sussex fly up to perch above her head—a welter of russet feathers burnished in the windows' grimed sunset. She sits on the floor, and they float down to chuckle at their rooting—a querulous sound. One bird gives a soft coo; another replies with a mutter.

Pea hens are old women, nattering
> *in a night*
>> *laundry, perhaps*
it is a darker sound:
They are the gossiping neighbors of
>> *a French peasant girl:*
"She's a witch, that hen is her familiar.
They cackle, those fowls—the unspeakable."

Stooping to leave the chicken coop, she stumbles, and finds herself on her knees in front of a hutch where a newborn albino rabbit lies on one side, its left leg in a splint. She opens the door and lifts it onto her lap.

The musk of fur, the dusty
rasp of feather, cage after cage
the animal eyes, the clutch of claw, the pads
on paws, the urine sodden sawdust, troughs
of hair-flecked water, pails of water for
litters of calico kittens. Animals are
what they are—a breathing and a silence.
Still
someone has kept the injured
rabbit in its mother's breast down.
Someone who has been watching tells her,
"That's your job now."

At dusk, She listens for the hooves against the door.

The horse on his hind legs—
as the forelegs fall
a tattoo, with lighter
strokes between the heavy on the wood—
splintering blows, a whusk, a
                    whimper-
ing, this horse intends
his legs
to mark the time.

When the hoof beats cease, she unbolts the door and goes out:

> *The white stallion owns the pasture.*
> *She knows she'd better hurry*
> *through the grass to safety*
> *in the discarded wagon and no sooner*
> *does she vault the rust and wood rot*
> *than he gallops to a halt before her.*
> *He snorts and turns away but she does not*
> *release him— all the night*
> *she draws him in*
> *a line of power,*
> *neck to flank. She draws*
> *his nostrils, seeing the pasture*
> *balloon in and out with his breath—*
> *mirage of his heat and her pen.*

53

WOMAN WITH CHRYSANTHEMUMS
by DEGAS

She leans back into petals
as she scans a milk glass sky.

Outside purple loosestrife
swallow the marsh.

The sparrows have left
along with the rue and cowslip.

Dreams of perfect transience:
Forever, she removes her gloves,

arranges dripping blossoms
to flicker in the vase.

She won't pinch the buds
between her fingers,

but feels them burn
behind her back.

TRANSPORT

A girl gets on the streetcar
holding a corymb
of lighted candles.

She leans to the flames—her face
leaps back from the flowers!

One old woman doesn't even see the shadow of a flame. She rides to the railroad station away from the Via Del Vecchio where her crumbling house slides downhill while her roomers laugh and drink wine in the kitchen. They know she plans to snare weary tourists. Even now the tourists count their luggage. Because they are uncertain, they are always ready: Their train may still be moving south. Or perhaps, it's only another—train speeding north across their window. Travel teaches their eyes to catch on light.

The old woman, still ten stops from her quarry, schemes so devoutly, her thoughts scraping together like two stuck coins in a kiosk automat, that at first she doesn't notice—the streetcar no longer stops! The other passengers hold tightly to the slatted wooden armrests. As the streetcar inclines into the river curve, they gaze at the girl:

Her seven flames fuse
in an arc below her chin.

Like dried seeds turning in a wax gourd,
transients keep the Shabbat with her:

In and out of windows, someone's garden.
and the dark streets tunneled by a rain south wind.

PORTRAIT OF AN OLD
HOUSEWIFE AS AN ARTIST

*An elderly artist has almost completed a series of minimalist paintings—all
numbers in sequence. Thirty years ago, he began with a black number one
on a black field. The positive and negative shapes have been gray a very long
time in their progress toward white where they will merge and his life's work
will be far too luminous for us to see. Even now his ground and figure near
the condition of light on light—a million.*

*The artist has carefully documented his process on videotape, itself a part
of the work of art. His voice can be heard counting as he paints. We view him,
but then she limps onto the screen as he paints time—*

> subletting his dust
> to his wife, and she drones,
> "Everyday it's the same
>
> beds to do—sheets take body
> shape when they're two weeks old.
> My life is as hard to alter as soft sculpture.
>
> Our walls refuse my paint,
> paper blisters. I must peel it.
> Like sunburned skin, it itches.
>
> A tug might hurt . . . stripping walls
> is my way in when I can't
> throw anything out at all."
>
> She throws days abutting days.
> This clay-slab woman lives
> uncollected. Soil reveals
>
> her life line—intaglio—
> the whorl on her thumb,
> her work. She shuffles

remnants in a circle
(shed/cellar/shed) unconnected.
Yet like the woman with thirty cats,

which have chosen her, she chooses
life—with an eye for uncut edges,
scraped between the nails

of thumb and forefinger,
torn then eased together,
in the method of collage.

THE OPENING

1.

I remember, a small child,
the first time my eyes
glaze over looking at a snail—

seeing my hand
and the grass below:

The curved shell fits my palm.
Inside the ribboned dead,
concentric skins pull away.

My fingers poke the crevice,
afraid to find moist
wormy life in the dark.

But this dry snail
unwinds in springy coil.
Did she crawl inside
and die of sun?

2.

Golf balls in those days:
rubber beneath dimpled sheaths
then miles and miles of string.

Lower is a smaller core
of acid—nips the fingers!

3.

I make nesting boxes of paper-mache
getting smaller, till only
my little finger fits.

I paint acorns and squirrels
on the outer walls,
feathers inside.

I start with a brush, and end
with just one hair for
the hummingbird's
egg.

4.

Hostas poke up white, each shoot
pierces loam, and thrusts
furled tight to
a point.

My pencil unwinds each
carbon-smudged line
as yellow leaves
loll back
to lime.

Soon
the tip of
my fat black brush
leaves a lush olive tongue.

5.

Holding the under-arch of each foot,
rock forward, in a trance
of drawing:
    the snail
    out of its shell,

the leaf falling
from my pencil—
a lace skeleton.

*Am I a snail,
do I unroll*

I am. I don't have to be

*my skin
from shell
to shell*

here, but I am here.

*or like the humming-
bird do I weave
my home?*

It's me. I make this.

6.

It's easier to weave, to thread the song
just below the surface of my breath
all the day toward night I
raise the warp beam
raise the griff bar
push the treadle
move the heddles
feed the weft
turn the spools
humming for
myself.

7.

I dream a room-sized box
for my thirty-third birthday present.
on the cover, moss grows
into a tiny jungle, then—
rapid time-lapse foliage.
I try to trick the growth
with a slow opening:

I can't go inside
unless I'm willing
to lose my garden.
Then slanting the door,
                    I gently
telescope the trees.

Inside I find a note for me:
*"Happy Birthday, Little Mother
on your painting exhibition."*

The work is mine,
arranged to show
the process of the making,
each picture taking deeper hue,
deep space contracting,
then expanding,
as if a light
came from each center,
in and out, then spreading.

· PRINTS FROM A REDUCTION BLOCK ·

In a reduction block, the artist works from light to dark, carving the same wooden block, and printing each color in turn, until nothing remains on the block but a pattern of black lines.

ABOUT TIME AND BUSES

Art does not compute and it's not
real time. Life, however, is a bus ride.

1.

One day I run for the bus with a suitcase full of tubes and turpentine and my breath rasps out in rage against all fugues and time-borrowings. My wet oil painting bumps against my chin. I'm too sick to sprint. A cyclist turns round on the bridge. What was more astonishing? That he gives me his bike or that I take it? As the bus leaves, I look back at the unchained bike and hope it's there for him. That is the first strange way I move on the bus that day.

2.

I have no fare. A lady gives me her transfer, but will not talk to me. Then the bus driver parks to address us for the last time he'll be taking us home on the 5:40 run. He's sorry and will miss us. That's nice, I think, though I'd never ridden with him before. It's too late for us.

3.

The drunk's voice comes on the bus before his hand-sloshing plastic beer. "Why you all just sitting there, whata buncha motor mothers," he says and sits next to me. To the boy and girl behind us: "Are you lovers? You must make real good love. You know she's a fox, doncha?" I feel the man's stare whining at me: "Why you so unfriendly? She won't look at me. She too good for me. She's no fox." I leave the bus five blocks before my stop. In a hurry-along, I hear his voice, "I'm here! I'm here! Look at me!"

4.

I board the next bus with a blind man and his wife. "After you, ladies," he says. "Thank you sir," I say and sit behind a man who sits alone yet speaks now and then to the package beside him. A woman says to the blind man's wife: "Tell your husband I like his suit." "She likes your suit," the wife relates, and he is amiable too.

I am out the door of the bus when the blind man calls for the driver to stop. "She forgot her painting!" It had jiggled with each turn against his knee. By 46th Street he knew it as well as I did. That is the last strange way I move on the bus that day.

FOR THOSE WHO ARE
LOST IN WINDOWS

This morning, while boarding the bus
                I lower my eyes
and sit in the first vacant seat.
A lady wants to sit on my parcels
so I move them, being careful
             not to look at her.

On the night trip, the windows
           reflect faces turned
to the ghosts of faces.
I walk past a man
like a memory

of someone's clay features.
From the corner of my eye, I see
his nose beak, his chin sharp.
his body jerk. He groans.

We all agree not to hear him, so
we can go on being public.
           I place my privacy
in the window—the orange mercury vapor
street light prints my face upon
an old woman, head down and angry.
Shuffle, gibber: Does she care
her misery is a howl out loud?

Sometimes I curse
           a growling litany
and know that I'm alone.
But there will come a day

when I won't know, flapping along
in my bedroom slippers
as my mouth works

on spit and imprecations:
like that sleep-walking dream—
losing the state of grace.

AN OLD MAN GOES SHOPPING

Clockwise crowds spin the old man. He pushes counter, mutters at the door that snaps his heels.

The phone rejects his quarter. A shopper tells him, "Pick up the receiver first." The old man watches his own hand to remember if he did that yet.

He signs with a smile to the young saleswoman. What he wants is hidden somewhere and he can't name it. But it soothes his throat to speak so he speaks on—of small shops, cardamon and sawdust, of the gypsies, cedar chests and caraway, of sage, paprika and pork.

She holds the right box at last, "Is this what you want?" He gestures yes and no, so she begins to take the pieces out. "Put together, it grinds food." He waits for her to tell him more, then shakes his head. She begins to turn the pages of a catalog. "Is this it? Is this?" At last she points to a sausage attachment. He moves to embrace her, but she says, "It must be ordered." He doesn't understand. He must think about this, so he goes.

He begins to come each day with every scrap the past tosses back to him: The old farmer from Lodsk, who fattened his geese on fermented wheat. As he speaks to her she feels consonants spike clusters of soft, fat vowels. She imitates his own palms-up shrug, "May I help you?" He turns away: She must already know his situation.

Ancient light: a window or other opening that has been used for twenty years or more and is therefore protected under common law against obstruction by an adjoining holder. (Landlords are building skyscrapers to his east and to his west.)

ANCIENT LIGHTS

He doesn't own
the room, the bed, the drapes—
bleached lighter, each window-side
fold for forty years.

He can't scrape the dust—
thick in waves to the bottom of
the west-pane wind flue,
trick of a narrow alley.

As if under water,
or through old glass,
sun slants, leaving
window-shaped patches,

faded carpet beneath
one chair he shifts
with the time of day,
north to south with the season.

He owns the ancient lights
from someone else's window.
If he appeared in court
(if he knew his rights),

he could submit his evidence—
the patch of faded carpet
and the sun-striped drapes
                    or his face.

"SNOWFENCE," INSTALLATION P.S. 1, NEW YORK
BY ELIZABETH BACHHUBER, 1988

THE SPECIAL INDULGENCE
OF MEMORY

*In fourth grade on All Soul's Day at Saint Pius,
we'd enter the church, genuflect, and say
a spell of Our Fathers and Hail Marys, saving
souls from purgatory. I forget how many.*

*We thought we'd waste time and dead sinners
going all the way home between visits, so
we kept going in and out the door.*

Now, I cannot ransom
Eric, who has no friends—
                What can I do
if he comes with his pocket knife,
and balks in our driveway, weeping,
                     and he wants
to play. He says he'll slice
the tires on our son's new bike:
                He wants to play.

And Gina with the layered face—
from her father, boiling water—
who'd bring her in when she
smokes dope. We must consider
children of our own.

Who'd wake up an ordinary day
and go out for a soul in Limbo.

If you can't remember someone
does he go away?

If we stopped to have supper at one hundred souls,
what about the rest?

What about Charlie Osgood
who raised eight brothers and sisters,
ironed their shirts, sent them to school
and died, an old bachelor, of drink,
alone in his one-bed sitter?

REDUCTION BLOCK

Acid rises in the teacher's throat,
on cigarettes, black coffee, morning
hurry to the classroom one hour early.
Peaceful. Children's drawings
climb the wall, shine
from the floor, the desks—just so.
    It's already past
the day they turn
as one child,
their backs to her
and scream one laugh.
The table with the paints
bends like the cow at Nazareth.
Colors slide and, low and slow,
she is still cleaning
the same stains, an endless
supply of crayons to crumble.
She hears her own voice,
    a thin hysteric
pale wash over black
action-painting criss-cross lines.

Good days: small people, surprised
     into making
something of their own.
All semester John pares his
reduction block, and at the end
saves the green and yellow with
a running boy above in black.
Proud, she displays a print
behind her desk, then finds
the others stuck together in his locker,
     and herself—
blurred through multiple tracings

on oiled paper in hot June,
cleaning the storage closet.
She will not come back. Her neatness,
commended by the fire marshall,
was the one thing she had not expected.

CASE HISTORY

Adam wears his pants too high.
Unable to mimic the gifted,
He nips at the edge of the classroom.

The school begs his glasses,
all the care he's likely to get
light years too late to read.

Safe, brutal children
snatch his windows—his
peeled eyes have no place to fasten.

His family isn't wooed with handmade,
four-months-in-the-making
Christmas presents.
It's known abused children
won't give up on their parents.

His mother took a turning in
post partum, hating sour
milk, then sleeping/waking
to count her feelings—
a few dried seeds.
His father has mean money.

The facts of his case
are stubborn as he is.

Seeing like the blind,
my fingers chalk his mischief.
I can't teach him
and would leave him
like his mother,
except for my anger.
My closing fingers can
compress the two-twig wrist bones.
Like his mother, I'm stunned
with wanting just to be.
My bones could burn to his bones.

His chatter is the ceaseless
needy echo of
her own, my own
hurt—
not to be enough
with nothing left for him.

It feels like love
to suffer this child
I can neither
tighten nor
loosen again.

HOW WE CAME TO LIVE
IN A CITY OF LOSS

In memory of our friend,
Herb Behrend,
New Orleans, 1972

That summer in our need,
heat made our bodies slip,
touching dark.

How often did we start,
sit up in bed
and he was gone—

in the space between the cry
that woke us and the next
we remembered

    The evening of the night
    he died, he invited us
    to enter his room,

    and we listened to Brahms:
    The contralto's lament
    moaned below a single flute,

    the bass, the plodding
    voices of the men, all unable
    to lead one wanderer home.

    But her voice flowed and wove
    the baritone and bass together
    like a rope, belaying them

    through that valley
    to the wasted foothills,
    and pulled them up the desolate

mountain, rising and falling,
                    an octave of
fierce tenderness.

The night he died
police cars
knifed through the empty

streets
all stoplights
fixed on red.

That day we looked
through rust
obscene scraps

spent rubbers
the grasses so high
they might cover anyone.

When they found him
our private grief
was taken from us with

his lopsided smile
we couldn't identify
the body   anyone's face.

By newspaper, his life
was judged by his end—
his beating, rape,
              his silence.

      ✳

In my dream he is still alive
always in his room and music.
A contralto sings Brahms's "Alto Rhapsody,"

singing pain, and she continues
past acceptance and the act.
He lifts his hand, conducting—

her last note down
to vibrate still in such a world,
and his waiting   life would heal.

QUICK

The spring her daughter moved back
to Gramma's upstairs city flat
with four raucous kids, it wasn't bad—
just crowded, till the summer, when,
with knees pushing out of blue jeans,
they hurtled down the stairs,
jostling like rude hollyhocks,
to the garden she'd tended
alone for twenty years.
She, absentminded,
looked up from her herbal
and the garden rushed by—
behind the children's moving limbs,
upside down from plum trees—
Canterbury bells following
close upon lupin, and phlox
exploded into cosmos—
streaked with a new blackened purple,
red, a slash of orange, and subsided.

All unfurlings
she used to notice separately
unrolled behind the children
as the garden waved, and grew in jerks,
like the background of a silent motion picture.
And the city horns, gratings, hot asphalt
didn't shrink, so much as deepen. Grass
was always ankle deep. Faster, faster
each four o'clock
opened at dusk and winked
out by morning, soft explosions,
leaving tiny spent knobs.
Then weeds sprang up, blurring
borders, hollow stems, flowers falling
into thistle, hard to see,
bleached from the center,

cataracts growing their isinglass
or just her age, her blood so low
that early autumn, when
the Gloriosa didn't die, but dried
mahogany and gold, and asters
fell in the order they sprouted
—but slow this time,
each frame caught: a small brown hand,
a knee, skinned, a dirty face. Her daughter,
this woman who smoked too much and didn't hum,
wiped the counters, table, stacked
her tasks like plates. Gram remembered—
When tending her own small children,
she watched a grape vine kill a spruce.
She hadn't time to prune it.

When they left, she tidied beds,
tied the wrist-thick vines,
dark curving veins,
to her chain link fence.

THE LIFE IS GREATER
THAN THE BODY:
In memory of our cousin, John Gross,
who died at twenty-one

for his parents, Frank and Jean

1.

"Indian John," his parents said—
the way his hands touched colored stones
or ships he made   in his tenth year,
every spritsail owned by him,
a world so small   it could be whole:
brigantine, sloop, or schooner—
naming them satisfied,
like poetry—a precise love.

2.

Initiation: Each day's journey
began when they found his cancer.
He had survival skills
and needed
to use what he knew:
rappel rock face, and make
bone-shelter, sure-foot edge
on the incline, blaze a trail
to leave the trees
undamaged.

Before the end he used
more than he knew.

3.

"We buried him with all those things he loved,"
his mother said, "not the finished
          but the incomplete—

like hiking shoes with many walks left in them."
She had an instinct for the ongoing:
A Navajo sandpainting
must be returned to sand
after the healing ritual.
If something is finished
        it's dead.

4.

In John's first year,
his mother painted butterfly fishing nets.
No sooner did she fix the masts,
rigging rope on spar,
than sails filled with air—
a flock of sea gulls,
filling her canvas with scallops of
sun, multiplied as many times as she
        laid her brush down,
and she was never finished.

5.

In John's last months,
he could only look
at sculptures he'd built
of handmade paper,
at a sketch in black Contșe of his cousin's arm,
done but not completed even though
        his own hand
once parted the air without resistance.

6.

Before he was sick, he began
a poem, lying on his back
in the middle of a gulley wash road
that snaked the woods all night.

As he lay upon the sand, he collected
small sounds, the breathing of deer,
crepitation of twigs or bones.

7.

The body of work John left
is small. As his body
grew smaller, his thumb print,
water mark, was raised
from the days of his life,
          compressed
then expanded like the stock
of his handmade paper—into the most distinct
layers: that camp with his father, found
by moon and compass, the way
martial arts he learned were something more
          than balance—
a fulcrum,
his enduring presence.

WHAT'S LEFT OF HOME

for Steve, Mary, Tom, and Nick

1.

Our family's from the Horicon Marsh,
not given to extremes, between
Lake Michigan and Lake Superior
          on the Rock River,
and near the Kettle Moraine.

No mountains, no waterfalls.
We looked neither down nor up, except
once yearly, when twelve thousand geese
sheared the farmers' corn on landing.

No one ever took a picture of the marsh
until half our family left,
              and one by one sent back
black clouds, silver wings, white fields.

2.

Setting our depth of field just short
              of infinity, we plumbed
the Black Canyon of the Gunnison—
deeper than we'd ever cared to go,
so high on the Leadville pass,
we lost our trust in maps.

Finding our way in the cross hairs
of the viewfinder, cutting peaks
to fit, and in the desert's
              immense light—
we stopped the camera down,

keeping each proof of the old
home, where the sky and wetlands
change places, forever upside down
in the retina of the family eye:

Folks who see one landscape
one hundred forty years,
take the afterimage with them—
vetch and duckweed on highway 94,
prairie's double-exposure
as if cattails burst open,
releasing white seeds, and the ruptured
                    long stalks pointed forward

as if one of Aunt Louise's
sweaters were unraveled, each row kinked
into the row before it and beyond it,
          then pulled taut.
The miles, the years, are like that.

EYES OF THE WINDOW MAKERS

Apprenticed at last
to the stained glass maker,

I was glad for craftsman's words,
and the movement of hands:

*To score the glass, you must
draw the cutter wheel toward you*

*in one steady line.
Protect your eyes.*

*To break the glass, your thumbs
press down, yet up and away,*

*So the halves fall cleanly
with that definitive snap.
Protect your eyes.*

What I hoped to gain
in permanence, I cannot say—

I only soldered joints
shiny and flat,

connecting lead
black lines to separate

pieces of sun
and make some difference with color.

"WATERFOWL I," INSTALLATION P.S. 1, NEW YORK
BY ELIZABETH BACHHUBER, 1989

Patricia Barone worked as a painter and printmaker in the 1960s and '70s, but for the last eighteen years she has been writing poetry and fiction. Her first book, *The Wind*, a novella, was selected as a winner of the Minnesota Voices Project and published by New Rivers Press in 1987. In 1989, a chapter of her unpublished novel was given a Lake Superior Contemporary Writer's Award. Barone lives along the Mississippi River with her family and works as a staff nurse in a nursing home.